# Sandtray Therapy

Everything You Need To Know To
Start Using Sandtray Therapy With Your
Clients Today

Michael Elliot, LCPC

Copyright © 2017 Michael Elliot

All rights reserved.

ISBN-13: 978-1979507639
ISBN-10: 1979507635

Copyright © 2017 by Michael Elliot

No part of this publication may be reproduced or transmitted in any form or by any means without the explicit permission in writing from the author or publisher.

The information in this book is not intended to be used as a substitute for professional help or training. The advice contained herein may not be appropriate for every situation. This book is sold with the understanding that that the author and publisher is not engaged in rendering psychological, or other professional services. If you believe you are in need of professional services or counsel, contact a competent professional person. Neither the Author nor the Publisher shall be liable for damages arising herefrom.

# TABLE OF CONTENTS

|   | FORWARD: SANDTRAY THERAPY MADE EASY | 1 |
|---|---|---|
| 1 | INTRODUCTION TO SANDTRAY THERAPY | 3 |
| 2 | THE FIRST SESSION<br>INTRODUCING SANDTRAY THERAPY TO THE CLIENT | 9 |
| 3 | THE STRUCTURE OF SANDTRAY INTERVENTIONS | 13 |
| 4 | DEEPENING THE PROCESS | 21 |
| 5 | WORKING WITH PARENTS | 41 |
| 6 | GROWING AS A SANDTRAY THERAPIST | 47 |
|   | APPENDIX: MAKING THERAPY WORK | 55 |

## AUTHOR'S NOTE

The case profiles described in this book are composites of typical client stories. Some stories have been combined or partially fabricated, names and other identifying details have been altered to protect the privacy of the individual.

## Sandtray Therapy Made Easy

Every therapist knows that to really reach our clients and help them achieve the deep transformational changes they need, it's not enough to just talk about it. Because emotional wounds happen at an experiential level beyond the realm of the verbal, healing also has to take place using non-verbal experiences. Sandtray Therapy is one of the most effective and powerful tools that any therapist can quickly learn and use with literally any client of any diagnosis.

When I first learned about the potential and promise of the expressive therapies, I never thought I would be able to actually incorporate them for my clients. I had looked into learning Sandtray Therapy, and discovered that most trainings go into great detail and seem to encourage therapists to basically convert from being a Talk therapist to a Sandtray Therapist. This entails buying hundreds, if not thousands, of miniatures, and multiple types of sand, and sand boxes, as well as redesigning your entire office to host the equipment. All this in addition to the lengthy and expensive trainings by experts.

This was more of a change than I was willing to make, especially because I just wanted something to be a helpful nonverbal tool in addition to traditional Talk Therapy.

Fortunately, I turned to a friend and colleague who

was a talented Play Therapist. She explained to me that even if you don't "convert" to being a Sandtray Therapist, just about any client can still benefit from even just a little bit of Sandtray. She gave me several impromptu lessons in the basics of Sandtray Therapy and my clients benefitted. Since then I have gradually gone on to take additional trainings and supervision. This book is my attempt to offer every clinician a brief yet sufficiently comprehensive introduction to Sandtray so that it can readily be incorporated into practice. What you read in this book is not supposed to be just an appetizer, although I hope you find it appetizing and inspiring to continue your development as a therapist in general.

In this book, I've made Sandtray Therapy available to any therapist who is genuinely interested with the minimum amount of commitment. I've outlined the three basic steps of every Sandtray Therapy intervention, as well as given some ideas of how you introduce Sandtray to your clients. Because Sandtray is non-verbal, it requires a different *language* when guiding clients, and so I put a special emphasis in the book to provide the reader with a lot of phrases that is conducive to this process.

I have no doubt that as you begin to use Sandtray in your practice, both you and your clients will be glad you did!

# 1

# INTRODUCTION

**What is Sandtray Therapy and how can you use it to help your clients and students to access and process their inner world?**

Sandtray Therapy is an expressive (non-verbal) intervention which helps individuals connect to their inner world and find solutions. Under the guidance of a therapist or teacher, the person uses a selection of objects to create a three-dimensional tangible expression of their emotions, thoughts, and beliefs. After a client is able to get it "out of their head" and put it out there in the world, they are often able to approach it and process it differently. The definition of Sandtray Therapy given by Homeyer and Sweeny in their book Sandtray Therapy: A Practical Manual is, "The therapeutic use of a collection of miniatures in a sandtray. It is a non-verbal expressive and projective mode of psychotherapy where the sandtray and the miniatures are the medium of communication. It is client led and the therapist is only the facilitator. The process seeks to promote safety and control for the client so that emotionally charged issues can be addressed utilizing the sandtray."

## What's wrong with just Talk Therapy?

Sandtray Therapy doesn't have to be a stand-alone therapy. Instead, it's usually employed as an adjunct intervention to Talk Therapy. Sandtray interventions can make Talk Therapy even better.

For many of our clients, words are not enough. Especially individuals impacted by negative experiences or dealing with intangible emotions, words simply cannot capture their experience. In cases of trauma, abuse, and neglect, client's often lose their ability to talk about the event without getting overwhelmed and retraumatized. For times like this, Talk therapy usually reaches a standstill where both client and therapist get frustrated. At times like this Sandtray therapy can be effective, making the process of therapy more empowering for the client and rewarding for the therapist. Carl Jung is quoted as saying, "Often it is necessary to clarify a vague content by giving it visible form…Often the hands know how to solve a riddle with which intellect has wrestled in."

## Who Can benefit from Sandtray Therapy?

Literally everyone, (including you).

Sandtray Therapy interventions are successful with both adults and children, and can be helpful with almost any diagnosis and treatment goal. Therapists can easily incorporate a Sandtray into their repertoire without extensive trainings so that their clients can benefit immediately.

Even though it is an expressive modality, it doesn't require a high degree of artistic talent whatsoever because the objects and miniatures are all prefabricated so that all the client has to do is arrange them the way they want. This enables all clients to access emotions through the use of their hands, creativity and their right-brains!

## Why Sand?

The items are put in the sand which holds them. However, there are several additional benefits to specifically using sand. Firstly, the sand itself is a manipulatable object that becomes part of the expressed environment. Clients can move around the sand to represent hills and valleys. The bottom of the Sandtray is blue to represent water, and clients often move the sand out of the way in the spots they want to show water. (This is not something you have to tell them, almost all clients figure it out on their own).

Secondly, the tactile stimulation of the sand is both

engaging and soothing. Some clients when invited to try the sandtray will spend a long time just dipping their hands in the sand and moving it back and forth. This is especially helpful for clients with dissociative features and survivors of trauma.

## What are other benefits of Sandtray for the therapist?

As a therapist, there's nothing more frustrating than seeing your client struggling with being stuck and not knowing how to help them. Sandtray interventions are easy to employ, and work at almost all stages of therapy.

Another benefit for the therapist is that when they add a tool like this to their repertoire, clients and referral sources recognize them as specialists and unique practitioners. This credibility puts you one up above credentials and that translates to a fuller practice and more money.

The best part about it is that it really sets the tone for therapy in general and is especially good at teaching clients the process of therapy. Often, clients seeking therapy for the first time, are not familiar with the idea of therapy and are hoping that the therapy will give them advice. It takes time for them to learn the style of self-reflection and process of exploration. Using Sandtray is a helpful tool that puts clients in touch with the experience of just exploring their inner world which makes their whole therapeutic process smoother. What could be more rewarding than helping your clients become actively involved in their therapy?!

## Is Sandtray just for children?

Definitely not! Sandtray can be used with children, teens, adults, and couples.

## Do Clients Have to Play?

Sandtray Therapy usually does not include the element of play. While it's true that child clients do naturally begin to play with their tray and that can be very useful, most adults do not. It's not just playing around in the sand!

# 2
# The First Session
# Introducing Sandtray Therapy to the Client

Once you see how powerful a simple Sandtray can be for your clients, you will want to try it with all of them. The most common hesitation that new Sandtray therapists express is that they think it sounds weird to describe to clients and are afraid they will be turned down or just sound odd. The truth is, most clients are both willing and curious to try it. The more you use it and get used to it yourself, you will gain confidence in introducing it to your clients.

However, to make it a little easier for you to get started, we've included a model script below of exactly what to say to your client the first time you're introducing it to them. This first session format is powerful in its own right, and also serves as a helpful introduction for the client to using Sandtrays in future sessions.

"I've recently learned about something that's really powerful, and I think it's something worth your experimenting with. It's called Sandtray Therapy, would you like hear about it?"

[Client usually says yes]

"It's actually pretty simple, and I bet you can even figure it out yourself. Before I say too much though, let me tell you some of the reasons I think it would be helpful. First, it helps *me* to understand you- to really get you. Second, most people find that it helps *them* access their story or situation in a different type of way which can help *you* open up solutions.

[Then, physically pointing out the sound tray and bringing it out] I've got this Sandtray over here which as you can see has some sand in it. Over there, I've got a whole bunch of objects that you can chose from. The way this works is you're going to take some of those items and set them up in the sandtray however you want. Want to give it a try?"

This is definitely not the only way to introduce it, and every person has to say it in a way that is truly theirs. I would like to emphasize below why the wording above was chosen so that when you craft your own introduction you can consider including some of these components:

1. **"Worth you experimenting with."**- This phraseology makes the sandtray feel less like an intervention, and more like an experience which is exactly what you are trying to offer your clients. Further, it purposely leaves vague the intent of the Sandtray leaving it up to the Client to 'experiment.' Introducing the client to this opportunity to experiment with the unknown serves a metaphorical purpose that can help the client get more comfortable with experimenting the unknown outside of the session.
2. **"You can even figure it out yourself"**- again, this phraseology suggests to the client that they have the ability to figure things out. This conveys to the client in a subtle way that the process of sandtray is actually quite intuitive and something they can do.
3. **"Before I say too much"**- It's important not to talk too much about exactly how the Sandtray will help. As with all non-verbal modalities, words can't completely convey the experience and you don't want to kill it by trying. Instead, the goal is to help the client have that experience himself.
4. **"Helps me understand you"**- Clients often doubt whether therapists actually care, and saying something like this communicates that you are truly interested in hearing the client and "getting them."

5. **"Help you open up solutions"**- In these words, you have set the context and expressed confidence that the client, not the therapist, will be able to find solutions to their problem. How empowering!

# 3

# THE STRUCTURE OF SANDTRAY INTERVENTIONS

There are three main parts of any sandtray intervention: the invitation, the processing, the closure. Below I define these three stages of a Sandtray session and give some specific examples of how to do them. Remember that even though I provide rationale for the specific language and wording in the interventions below, it is not to be followed strictly. Instead, the reader is advised to learn the ideas and principles from these examples and then apply them in a way that fits their natural therapeutic style.

**Stage I: The Invitation**

The Invitation is how the therapist presents the Sandtray intervention to the client and helps him transition from a talking mode to an expressive mode using the Sandtray. The reason it's called the invitation is because the therapist is never prescribing it nor insisting on it. Remember that Sandtray is not a repairing technique like Cognitive Restructuring, and therefore isn't something that can just be taught or demonstrated to a client.

Instead, Sandtray is a style of communication that allows the client to be curious, creative, and expressive about their inner world. Doing so often leads to healing either through being able to access and express difficult emotions or through developing solutions after seeing them. By inviting the client, and not pushing it, you convey a belief in their ability to approach their experience and deal with it in an effective way!

When you invite the client to do a Sandtray, you want to consider how suggestive you want the invitation to be. Just like in Talk Therapy, you may use open ended questions, or more specific questions, so too in Sandtray therapy. No matter what your therapeutic orientation is, you can use it within the Sandtray context. Below I give examples of how you may 'translate' Talk therapy interventions into a language compatible for Sandtray therapy invitations:

Client says: I'm kinda stuck. I always wanted to go back and finish school, but I know my husband needs me at home. But then again, that doesn't make me want to stop myself, I still want to go back. I don't know. I'm just stuck and it makes me anxious.

| Therapeutic Intervention | Talk Therapy | Sandtray Therapy |
| --- | --- | --- |
| Open Ended | Tell me more about your indecision about pursuing this career and the role your husband plays in it. | Can you create an image of this dilemma in the sandtray to give me some perspective on it? |
| Interpretative | You seem conflicted between pleasing your husband vs. finding a rewarding career for yourself. | I wonder if you might make a scene in the Sandtray of this conflict between wanting to please your husband vs. pursuing a rewarding career? |
| Emotional | How does that feel like- being stuck? | What does "stuck" look like? Can you show you me in the Sandtray? |
| Deepening the Experience | I wonder if you can tell me what you mean by "anxious"? | Which item from the miniatures can represent "anxious"? |

| Therapeutic Intervention | Talk Therapy | Sandtray Therapy |
|---|---|---|
| **Diffusing from Emotion/ Experience** | How do you feel about the stuck part of you? | Show me an item that could represent the feeling of angry and then place it in the Sandtray…<br><br>[Client selects an item and places it in box]<br><br>Now, select an item that represents you and place it in the Sandtray wherever seems right. |
| **Ego-State Work** | How does the part of you that wants to go to college feel towards the part of you that wants to be home for your husband? | Let's use the items in the Sandtray to show me how the part of you that wants to go to college feels towards the part of you that wants to be home for your husband. |

Effective Language for inviting clients to Sandtray:
1. Make a scene that…
2. Show me…

3. Set it up visually...
4. Can you use your hands to make this more tangible for me... [emphasizes the experience of making the intangible into the tangible].
5. Do you want to do a Sandtray about this?
6. What does this look like?
7. Create a world in the Sandtray that represents this...
8. Let's put this idea in the Sandtray... [particularly a good expression to use when facilitating the client to "step back" from their situation and assume an observer position]

## Stage II: Processing the Sandtray

There are two main interventions at this Processing stage: reflection, and guiding. The first is just to be reflective with and help the client "take in" the three dimensional expression they have made. The objective with this is to convey to the client that you as a witness are in fact observing their world. Additionally, you are facilitating their own shift in experiencing and expressing their world. The second type of intervention is guiding their process along towards a resolution or deepening it.

Below, you will learn some great ways of helping client's process their Sandtray so that they can gain a different perspective on themselves and find solutions to their problems.

**Reflection:** Usually it's just describing what you see without judgment or interpretation; may include asking

the Client to describe parts of the Sandtray or the whole thing.
1. I noticed that you choses several animals and placed them behind the fences…
2. I'm curious what you can tell me about these animals behind the fence?
3. Hmm, what going on over here? [pointing to animals]
4. This animal is looking in a different direction than the other animals…
5. So, what can you tell me about this world?
6. Where are you in this Sandtray?
7. Do you like the way it is or do you want to make any changes to the world you made here?
8. What do you notice about it?
9. What do you feel looking at it?

**Guiding:** Usually offering interpretation, or guiding client to offer interpretation
1. How did these animals get behind the fences?
2. Who put the animals behind the fences? Was it hard for him? Why did he do it?
3. Do you think the animals are happy there?
4. It seems like there's a story here. Can you tell me the story of what's going on here?
5. If things were to improve just a little bit, show me how that would happen.

6. Try taking a few steps back, and let notice what that feels like.
7. Try moving to the other side of the sandtray and see how that changes the feeling a bit. What do you notice?

Once you try out some of these interventions, you will see that it is very natural and very powerful. Your clients will thank you!

## Stage III: Closure

The last task and stage of every Sandtray session is closing the Sandtray session or intervention in a way that honors what it represented.

Remember that for clients, the Sandtray they create represents their inner world and so clients can feel a variety of different reactions to having to deconstruct their world and put away the miniatures. At the same time, putting away the pieces also can be a positive experience which helps clients integrate that although the metaphor of the Sandtray is being put away, their inner world which created it, remains intact.

Below are some guidelines that can foster a successful end to the Sandtray intervention:
1. Give a five-minute heads up because it can take time to put the items away
2. Take a picture of the Sandtray and offer to email it to the client (If you're willing to print a copy, even better!)

3. Ask the client which pieces they want to put away first
4. Assure them that if they want to make the Sandtray again, they can do so.

Try to budget in enough time at the end of the session to talk about the sandtray after it is put away. Although you already facilitated the client's processing during the Sandtray intervention itself, there's an added benefit of talking about it after it's put away as it helps integrate the experience into a verbal- and non-representational- way.

# 4

# DEEPENING THE PROCESS

The process of creating and engaging in a Sandtray for the client is a fascinating engagement with many levels and dimensions. In this section, I would like to outline two major components of almost every Sandtray engagement: Personal Empowerment and The Creative Process. Part of the power of Sandtray is that it is non-verbal and therefore can only be experienced. Therefore, my attempt to put into words these components will mean a lot more to the reader after they have had their own hands-on Sandtray experience.

## Component One- Personal Empowerment

We live in a Left-Brain culture which emphasizes and applauds success in Cognitive and Verbal achievements and academics. The truth is, that even within our culture, a lot of success isn't truly determined by the Left-brain but rather by the creativity and expression of the Right-Brain- or more accurately, the integration of both of them together. Nonetheless, acknowledging this at a cultural level is still insufficient and there exists a reluctance that many people have to allowing themselves to acknowledge and connect with their more expressive side. For this reason, clients will often start a Sandtray scene in a state of Confusion or ambiguity. They will say things like, "I just don't know what to do, or what pieces to pick." Some clients may put it on you when they say, "What do you want me to do? How should I set it up exactly?"

Remember that both the scene in the Sandtray and the creative process of constructing that scene are metaphors for your client's experience in life outside of the session. In life, we are often, in fact daily, faced by challenges that ask us to produce solutions, and there is an anxiety of not knowing where to begin or from where to draw a response. The Left-Brain searches desperately for a logical and objective answer. Of course, there often is none. Those with a background in Existential thought will appreciate this as one of the core existential dilemmas; of course, those with a life experience of self-reflection will also readily recognize this as familiar. Tolerating this anxiety of Non-knowing is actually the bridge that connects a person to their own generativity and problem-solving ability that emerges from their Right Brain.

John Keats, the Romantic English poet of the 19th Century, suggested that the key to accessing creativity was honing a skill he termed Negative Capability. He wrote, "I mean Negative Capability, that is when man is capable of being in uncertainties, mysteries, doubts, without any irritable reaching after fact and reason." According to Keats, the capacity to tolerate the ambiguity of life being uncertain energizes creativity and the ability to imagine new perspectives.

The first task for the client is to pass through, not avoid, the anxiety of Non-knowing and enter a state of Creativity and Expressiveness.[1] Upon beginning any Sandtray, clients experience a modicum of this existential anxiety with the task of creating a Sandtray, and yet not quite having any idea how to do it.

It's crucial at this point to not give in to the reflex to "save" the client by offering directives because by doing so you are robbing her of an opportunity to experience this anxiety and using it to tap into her creative resources. Instead, consider ways that you may be able to facilitate the client's accessing her inner-reservoir of creative energy. If you can help your client experience this shift in the session, she will be more likely to make

---

[1] I use the word "state" intentionally. Those experienced with working from a hypnotically-informed perspective will observe that the client is literally in a different state of mind as soon as they begin to engage in constructing a scene. From a neuroscience perspective, different neural networks are engaged during the creative process as I describe later in this section.

this shift in her life. Below I offer some suggestions to illustrate how you as the therapist can assist the client to cross the bridge of anxiety from Non-knowing to Creating.

This ability to face life's challenges from a place of confidence and creativity, requires proactively looking for resources to solve problems in a flexible way. I have come to refer to this as Personal Power because it is the power that emerges from within the person to respond to the otherwise overwhelming nature of Life. However, several of my clients who identify as religious relate better to the idea of being an "Empowered Person" because this term signifies that their own power is sourced in a Higher Power. From both personal and clinical experience, I believe that the two most important qualities that help a person access their own inner creativity in order to become an Empowered Person are Permission and Possessivity.

Below I describe these two qualities and how you can use them in session to help your clients develop them.

**Permission**

Giving clients permission to explore their thoughts and feel their feelings with the acceptance that they are not judged or deemed bad is one of the common factors that makes all therapies work. Consider from your own experience that most of the challenges with which people enter therapy are at some level related to an internal message that they are "not ok" or not acceptable in some way. At some level, clients relate that they don't feel they are permitted to be themselves. Much of the pain people describe from their childhood that remains with them until old age is the feeling that they are supposed to be a certain way, and that otherwise they simply aren't good enough. The way many children and adults manage their anxiety around these injunctions and the fear of abandonment that comes with them, is they learn to suppress their own desires and experiences in order to show a more favorable side. Of course, while this works in the moment to make them feel safe from abandonment, it hurts in the long term because it creates a sense of not being acceptable if they are authentic.

A major objective of most therapies is to help the client access a more authentic self and meet it with acceptance. Sandtray interventions are an excellent way to do this because of their projective nature which allows clients to access their inner feelings without getting blocked by their habit of suppression which often comes in the form of verbal defenses. For this reason, it is extremely important and opportune for the therapist to guide the Sandtray process by giving a lot of Permission to the client.

The only way to truly convey permission to a client is to deeply and genuinely believe that each person is acceptable the way they are and worthy of making their own choices. If you believe this, it will ultimately come across. However, because clients, like most of us, are so used to messages from others in their lives that convey non-acceptance, it's helpful to be explicit in your interventions to really express this acceptance to clients. One effective way to do this when using Sandtray techniques is to always ask their permission before doing anything. Below are some common phrases you may use throughout the Sandtray processing. I separated them into two categories that together makeup Permission: Freedom to choose, and Acceptance.

**Freedom to Choose**

"Would you like to do a Sandtray?"

"Would you like to choose some more, or put some back?"

"If at any time you want to put away some of the pieces you chose, or get some more from the shelf, you can feel free to do that."

"If you would like, you can set up the pieces in the sand. Of course, you don't have to."

"I'm curious if there's a particular aspect of the scene you created that you might want to share with me."

**Acceptance**

"Everyone does it differently, so there's really no

rules, feel free to choose whatever miniatures you want."

"You can choose whatever pieces you want, but you may begin to notice that you resonate with certain pieces, and something about them talks to you."

"You are doing great, something inside you knows exactly what to do."

"A lot of different things can come up for us when we make our scenes, whatever comes up for you is perfectly fine, and worth exploring."

"It's not uncommon to wonder if you are supposed to set it up a certain way. So allow me to say that there is no right or wrong way, as long as it works for you."

Can you see the potential of Sandtray? You don't have to preach to clients about their own self-worth, instead you have a real in-vivo opportunity to provide these corrective experiences! The above phrases are not to be memorized, but should serve as a way to help you develop skills to use in your own language when working with your clients. The guiding principle behind these phrases is Permission which we described as being comprised of Freedom to choose and Acceptance.

The second quality that enables a person to move through Anxiety of Non-knowing to being an

Empowered Person is Possessivity. In a way, Possessivity is related to Permission, and for that reason I describe it here after the section of Permission. Possessivity refers to the fact that each person is the owner of his life and self. Personal power comes from a sense of personal responsibility in your life.

Responsibility is a touchy subject because on the one hand it represents a person's maturity and stature in life, yet on the other hand many clients come in with the wounds of being attributed responsibility in a way that limited their Permission to be themselves. For example, they were responsible to always be happy and not upset their mother, they were responsible to become a lawyer when they really wanted to be a musician, or they were responsible to not be a burden to others or to not tell anyone of the abuse they suffered. Some adapt by taking on too much responsibility while others adapt by unshouldering all responsibility.

I believe it's important to understand that there are two types of responsibility: Responsibility that comes from being *obligated* to others, and Responsibility that comes from ownership. While both aspects of responsibility are important and play a role in healthy development and living, in this section I emphasize the importance of Responsibility of Ownership because it is often neglected and yet supremely important.

Paying taxes is something for which you are responsible to do because of your obligation to others;

however, mowing your lawn is something you are responsible for because of your ownership of your property. I remember the experience I had when I moved out of a condo and into my own house. On the one hand, I was overwhelmed with responsibilities I never had before. However, it felt worth it and empowering because I now owned my own property and felt privileged to be responsible for it.

An important lesson one needs to learn in life in order to access Personal Power is that they are responsible for their own life because it is theirs and no one else's. On the one hand, there is an added anxiety of responsibility for you own life because you can't just blame others or shirk responsibility on others. On the other hand, because you are the owner of your life, you don't have to receive permission from others to live on your terms, feel what you feel, think what you think, or be who you want to be.

Recognizing ownership of your life means to take possession of your self and life which empowers you to be authentic and true to yourself. This empowerment is what gives you and your clients the force to face the anxiety of Non-knowing and access your *own* creative resources.

By giving permission to your clients to engage in Sandtray you are implicitly *giving them ownership* of their session and choices. Now, you understand why it is so important not to give too many directives to the client in how to create a Sandtray scene. When you relieve the client's anxiety by directing them exactly how to make their sandtray, you have robbed them of the opportunity to dig deep and personal finding a solution on their ***own***. Instead, allow the client the moments they need to come up with their own expression this way the Sandtray becomes theirs.

One way to convey Ownership to the client when facilitating a Sandtray intervention is to offer them to take a picture of the Sandtray. You may say something like, "Would you like to take a picture of it to keep? After all, you created it, and it's yours." Another way to do this is ask them if they want to name their work of art. Naming something signifies their having possession over it.

Many new Sandtray therapists are nervous that "it may not work." First of all, even if it may not work out, it's worth risking it by doing it in a way that offers empowerment and ownership to the client. Second of all, on a more personal note, in my experience, it has *never* not worked. Clients, even the most skeptical, have always come up with their own creations and shifted from Non-knowing to Creatively doing.

**Component Two- The Creative Process**

Sandtray therapy is a powerful way to connect the client to the creative process. A brief internet research for what the definition of creativity is usually yields two results. The first is that creativity is about finding *new connections between old things*. The second definition is that it refers to producing something new. I would like to suggest an alternative third definition that resonates at an existential level as well as offers valuable clinical utility.

The creative process is not just about producing something new- neither in connections nor in outcome- but refers to the process of producing something that comes from the one creating it. That is to say, a creative endeavor is one that seeks to produce something that has no previous source other than the one it emerges from in the moment. When defining creativity like this, the creative process is the process of producing something that expresses the self of the person creating it.

Consider what Brendon Burchard writes in his book *The Charged Life*, "There are two things that change your life: either something new comes into your life, or something new comes out of you." Creativity is that second way of creating change in your life, a way that is an act of self-determination. In the section above, we described how there is a human tendency to search for ways of dealing with life's challenges by looking outside of ourselves and unfortunately there's not always a solution to be found. Creativity is not the search to find the solution within us, but giving up on finding it anywhere and instead opting to create it. In this way, creativity is not just about something new and novel, but rather a true expression of self-determination and responsiveness in the face of life's challenges.

In the book, What Matters Most, acclaimed Jungian analyst James Hollis describes "In general, we suffer from the fear of 'overwhelmment' and 'abandonment'. Although humans are weak, you should have your own will and not simply listen to others." Hollis prescribes "having your own will" as the solution to fear of overwhelmment that is the general cause of our suffering. The only shortcoming of this prescription is that it is impossible to have your own will when the world is truly more powerful than you. How can a young woman facing a terminal diagnosis find comfort in her "own will" to live? How can one who has lost a loved one- or lost anything for that matter- take comfort in his "own will" to have their beloved back? The truth is that in developing one's own will, you are forced to negotiate and compromise with the reality of life. This negotiation of refining your will in a way that will work with the world and yet still preserve it as being your will is part of resilience and part of life.[2] I believe that the creative process is at the crux of this negotiation with life.

So what is the creative process? The creative process

---

[2] This negotiation was described almost poetically is the words of Viktor Frankl in his book Man's Search for Meaning. He writes, "Between stimulus and response there is a space. In that space is our power to choose our response. In our response lies our growth and our freedom."

is characterized by allowing your mind to wander and imagine new possibilities uninhibited by fear of criticism or failure. According to Scott Barry Kaufman, author of Wired for Creativity, recent research indicates that this process is associated with increased activity in what he calls Imagination Networks of the brain which is located deep inside the medial region and is distinct from the prefrontal cortex. What this means for us is that when using Sandtray or any other medium of engaging the creative process, we are helping the client go beneath the "thinking" part of the brain, and giving them direct access to experience unconscious processes deep in their psyche.

Throughout life, every person at some point or another experiences distress, pain and loss. As we mature, we use our pre-frontal cortex to "think" our way out of the distress by recognizing that we are safe and fine. However, beneath the surface of this rational thought, we still feel the same pain and injury, it's just hard to access because our rational brain tells us not to worry and the pain remains, albeit unconsciously. For this reason, Talk Therapy is often not enough to access this distress. However, because Sandtray therapy is engaging the client in the creative process which goes deep beneath the rational mind, almost every scene a client creates reflects some element of unresolved pain, loss or emotional wound and allows the client to access it consciously. Long before the intricacies of Neuroscience made these discoveries, Carl Jung made the same observation and phrased it like this: Often the hands will solve a mystery that the intellect has struggled with in vain.

Once the client starts choosing the items that resonate with her, and then begins setting them up, the meaning this scene has begins to emerge from the unconscious and into the light of awareness. The creative process doesn't stop here, instead, the process continues with the ability for the client to then interact with this emergent unconscious material in a conscious way.

This is a process that happens with every scene in Sandtray. For example, first the client picks out some pieces simply because they like them at a visceral level. Often, while the client is choosing the pieces, they have no idea how the pieces are connected or what they are going to do with them. Then, the client is forced with the challenge of setting them up in a way that makes sense to them. They begin to either understand what the pieces and their positions mean, or they make meaning of it. Then, based on that meaning making, they interact with pieces and the scene in a way they couldn't have before, because they have already created something new that wasn't there before.

This process unfolds automatically as long as the person is staying present and engaging in their Sandtray. The role of the therapist is to guide the client in staying engaged with the scene by reflecting on the meaning it has for them, and then providing the client the opportunity to deepen the level of how they engage with it creatively. Both these tasks of Meaning Making and Deepening the Experience occur mainly in the Processing stage of the intervention.

## Making Meaning

Helping the client reflect on what the Sandtray scene represents to them is the first task. These questions are usually exploratory, and stated in a speculative way without giving much interpretation so as to allow the client to attribute their own meaning to what they have created. The following questions are often helpful:

"Tell me a little about what's going on in here…"

"Is there a part of this scene you can tell me a little more about?"

"I see you chose put a pretty large fence right in the middle, does that have any meaning for you?"

"Are you in here somewhere?"

"What is the relationship between this horse and this sea-shell?"

"It looks like these two people are facing opposite directions, can you tell me if that speaks to you in some way?"

## Deepening the Experience

The next task of the therapist is to assist the Client in engaging in the next level of the creative process. Remember, I have suggested that true creativity is when you produce something that emerges from the self. At this stage you want to deepen the connection the client has to their scene by moving beyond the meaning they attribute to it, and actually claim it as an expression of self. The task here is to help them identify the scene as reflecting their inner world, and then allowing them to interact with it as their own. The therapist should go about this stage quite slowly because it is important to give honor to the quality of emotion that emerges for the client at this stage. It is also important because often times at this stage a lot of raw emotion can come up, and it's important to titrate and support the emergence of the emotions so that the client can contain them in a healthy way.

Another word to the wise, before I begin this stage with a client, I usually explain it to them so they understand that I am understanding what they are going through. This allows me to be a witness for them, and also enables me to convey empathy for them. I usually say something like this, "Every scene a person makes is truly an expression of them. There is no one piece in here that is You. Instead every piece represents a part of you, and the scene as a whole also represents a part of You. For that reason, it is really yours and I need to ask your permission before we go on. Would it be ok if I offer you a little guidance here, and perhaps even help deepen this experience for you?"

If the Client says, "no," this is great because it means that they have already resonated with something in the scene and are choosing to claim their ownership over it by keeping it private. If they say, "yes," then I may say something like this, "Ok, and if at any point something comes up for that you are open to sharing, I am really curious to listen. Of course, on the other hand, the purpose is really for you, and you have the right to kind of notice it and keep it to yourself if you'd like."

Below I have included several example ways the therapist can employ to help the client personalize their Sandtray scene. However, this stage is highly intuitive and should really only be done after the therapist has gone through their own Sandtray process with an experienced clinician.

"Are there any pieces here that have something to say to you?"

"Are there any pieces here that you have something to say to them?"

"If you could shrink down into miniature size and enter your scene, where would you go? If I could go there with you, where would you want me to go and what would you want me to say?"

"This scene is really beautiful... You are really beautiful."

"I can really get a sense of the turmoil in this world... of the turmoil inside you."

"If there was something that this piece needs to hear in order to feel safe, what would it be? How about you actually say it now to this piece."

"In this scene, you said that this piece represents you as a child. Do you think this child knows about you right now as an adult? If not, would you like to let her know that she'll be ok? If so, would you like to let her know right now?"

"What do you notice you feel in your body as you observe what you're seeing about yourself in this scene?"

"Is there anything you would want to change in this scene that would be even just a little improvement? Would you like to change that right now, or does it feel right to keep it the way it is?"

"Is this piece which you said is the part of you that holds your pain from marriage aware of this piece which you said holds your hope? If not, do you want them to be aware of each other?"

## Summary

In this section, we have covered the major components of what makes the process of Sandtray therapy so powerful and useable for almost every Client in therapy. The first component is that it experientially promotes Personal Power- or the Empowered Person- which we defined as having Self-acceptance, Permission to be, and a sense of ownership in your own life. The second component is the fluid Creative process in which the Client engages with the Sandtray scene in a way that makes it personal and an expression of their self. This allows the client to experience the scene in a deeper and self-reflective way. The Therapist's role is to guide the client in these processes by serving in the role of compassionate witness, as well as guide the client in staying with the creative process and ultimately connecting to their creation.

Michael Elliot

# 5

# WORKING WITH PARENTS

One of the keys to successful work with children clients is to work successfully with the parents as well. As a therapist or teacher, you are only working with the client one or two hours a week, but the parents are with the client for the lion's share of the time. Moreover, any intervention that can help the parents be better parents will help the children thrive! I have found that using the Sandtray can be utilized to guide parents in developing their skills with their children. To be sure, what I describe in this section is not a classic Sandtray intervention because it is not an Expressive therapy intervention. Nonetheless, because it is a great utilization of the Sandtray and miniatures, I have included it here hoping the reader will benefit from it as much as I have.

The first thing you want to decide on is what skill

you want to teach the parents. This could be specific skills such as listening and reflecting or skills based abstract ideas such as parenting from a Growth Mindset. Alternatively, you may use the Sandtray experience just to foster a positive interaction between child and parent. Exactly what agenda you choose to teach the client or her parents depend on the individual case, and are beyond the scope of this book which is to introduce you to using Sandtray interventions, and therefore I leave that to your clinical judgment and experience.

For the sake illustration, let's take an example of wanting to teach parents to be more Mindful in their parenting. After discussing with the client's parents the purpose and importance of Mindfulness you extend the discussion to a specific skills in Mindfulness such as Non-judging Acceptance. In Mindfulness-based Therapies, Non-judging Acceptance refers to assuming an observer role, without getting involved to change something, but instead just noticing it for what it is.

The second step, after having discussed and decided on a specific skill you will focus on with the parents, it's important to make it applicable with the parents by discussing exactly how they can apply this with their child at home. This accomplishes two things. Firstly, it makes it seems less like you are preaching to them, and more like you are teaching and empowering them. Remember, parents can feel blamed for their child's challenges and by talking to them about the importance of Mindfulness, it can be perceived as blaming them for having not been accepting enough in the past. By giving specific examples of how they can use it in their organic environment (at home), it helps emphasize that you are not trying to blame them but rather help them. Secondly, it is hard to implement abstract ideas when they are new. Therefore, by developing concrete operations and actions that parents can do, you help them begin translating the abstract into the practical.

The third step is the step that involves using the Sandtray. Invite the parents if they are willing to engage in their child using the Sandtray as an exercise or training medium. The best way to do this is to tell the parents that you are going to do it first as a demonstration for them, but you would like them to try as well so they can get the hang of it and also to get a chance to be coached in it by you. In this step, you ask the child if they want to play with the Sand and miniatures. (I can't remember a single time a child under ten responded negative to this invitation).

During this step, your task is to use the targeted skill as much as possible. Let's use the example above where the therapist and parents established the goal to work on Mindful parenting, and the specific skill of non-judgmental observing. As the child is engaging in free play, make a lot of "Noticing" comments. For example: "Oh, I noticed you are taking a lot of pieces with the color blue… That digger truck seems separate from the rest of the trucks... I see you are really working hard at protecting the farm animals... Hmm, I notice that the dog is buried next to the house... You look like you are trying to make the tree standup in the sand but it's not working."

After doing this, or even as you are doing this, with the child, you are describing the process to the parents and you may say something like, "Obviously, a part of me wants to just grab the pieces from her and stand up the tree for her, or explain that she needs more sand to make it stable, but right now I'm just working on noticing. I'm even holding myself back from helping her, because even that is a form of judgement."

Now, invite the parents to do join their child and take over for you. As they begin to do it, you want to take the opportunity to guide them and support them- especially if they are doing it right! What's great about this type of intervention is that it really has a great carry-over into the client's and family's home life.

In the name of clarity, let's consider an example of targeting a specific parenting skill not related to an abstract concept like Mindfulness. Let's say that with the parents you defined a target skill to be "the broken record." The Broken Record is a parenting skill of repeating a rule over and over again without raising your voice or intonation despite a child's defiance. Often, when a child refuses to listen to parents, the parents respond to the child's defiance by raising their voice, threatening, or offering incentive to the child to comply. The result is that the in the short term, the child complies; however, in the long-run the child learns to rules are optional. Using the Broken Record, the parent simple repeats the original rule, without changing their tone of voice or responding to the child's attempts at defiance. To the utter shock of most parents, the child eventually listens without having to fight.

The way you may introduce parents to this using the Sandtray is you invite the child to start playing with whatever toys he wants. Then, as the child is doing something, you explain softly that although he can play however he wants, there are some rules, and he's breaking on. For example, you may say, "Sorry, but today there is a rule that you can't bury the stones."[3] If the child listens, you give him recognition and a compliment. However, if the child does not comply, you repeat the instruction the exact same way in a calm voice until he does comply. Then, you follow his compliance with a compliment.

The main purpose of using the Sandtray in this way is not for the therapeutic value it has in the moment, but more for the hands-on learning experience. In this way, you are taking advantage of Sandtray as being experiential and metaphorical, despite the fact that it's

---

[3] Usually, you don't need to think of something arbitrary such as "no burying stones." Instead, the child may already be doing something that needs instruction, such as playing with the sand outside of the box, or not wanting to put items away.

not expressive. To make things simple, let's summarize the steps above:

1. Define and establish target skill or concept
2. Specify concrete actions and operations how the parents can use this at home
3. Use the Sandtray as an experiential learning experience to both demonstrate to the parents and provide them the opportunity to train in the targeted skill

# 6

# GROWING AS A SANDTRAY THERAPIST

You will learn quickly, even the most basic interventions can help your clients make powerful transformations. As you use it more, your clients learn to get more comfortable with expressive experiences, and the benefits from one session to the next begin to compound. The introduction in this book is only the beginning and you may want to take your practice to the next level. For some, just using the Sandtray as an auxiliary modality will be enough. For other practitioners, there are several online trainings available in addition to many on-site trainings all over the world. There are many levels of advanced trainings that the interested therapist can pursue.

## Purchasing your First Sandtray and Collection of Miniatures

Getting started is easier than ever.

It used to be very difficult for anyone to gain entrance as a Sandtray Therapist because collecting a comprehensive inventory of miniatures was difficult, time-taking, and prohibitively expensive. Moreover, the tray itself is supposed to be blue to represent the sky and water and purchasing such a tray was almost impossible without spending hundreds of dollars to get something custom made. There were some start-up kits already available online, but after having reviewed them, it turns out their quality of items and selection were not professional. The last issue was that most therapy rooms aren't big enough to have a large tray and stand.

For these reasons, becoming a Sandtray Therapist used to be too big of a commitment for the average therapist and unfortunately, this incredibly simple and powerful tool was not available to the average client.

Did I mention how enthusiastic I am about Sandtray? For this reason, I collaborated with a team of Trauma experts and Sandtray therapists and together we created an affordable option to allow any therapist to immediately begin using Sandtray therapy with their clients. We packaged together a fully comprehensive Sandtray Therapy starter kit that includes all the miniatures, professional grade sand, and blue plastic tray that can be purchased at an affordable price. The best part is that we were able to keep it small and portable so it can fit in any office and even be transported easily.

The size of the actual Sandtray that you purchase depends on many variables including how much space you have in your office, whether you need it to be portable, and your budget for purchasing one. Because of the way that Sandtray works, the size of the tray doesn't seem to make a significant therapeutic difference. For those that wish to upgrade, there is a larger size blue plastic tray available for purchase.

If you are ready to upgrade the level of your practice to the next level and provide your clients with the ability to access and heal their traumas, then the EZ Sandtray Therapy Kit is a great place to start. It's available on Amazon and can be used right away.

Buying the startup items for a sandtray is definitely an overwhelming task. There are some logistical challenges such as how and where to find all the items you want, and there is also the stress and anxiety of not knowing which items you need. It is common in Sandtray Therapy trainings to quote that "the ideal collection of sandtray miniatures is everything in the world, everything that ever was, and everything else." Of course, this is also impossible.

This practical difficulty deters many therapists from ever trying, for fear of not being able to get it together. When I first learned about the power of Sandtray, I wanted to put it in my office immediately so my clients could begin benefitting from it and I could deepen my training. The problem was, as I began to buy items to build a collection, I saw quickly that I had no idea which items would be valuable. I wanted a list to follow so I could be confident that I had enough items to begin. I struggled a lot because I wasn't ready to invest a lot of money because I didn't have the confidence that I was getting the right items. I didn't want the challenge of logistics to prevent me from bringing it in my office because I know that perfectionism leads to procrastination which leads to me never doing things.

In addition to making it easier for you by including a list below of what I have found to be a sufficient startup collection of miniatures, I also want to offer an important insight that will hopefully relieve some pressure for you as a beginning Sandtray therapist. It is a common concern that your collection is not comprehensive, and worry, "Oh no, what if I don't have the item my client needs?!" Relax, the client can usually harness their creative capacity to compensate for this. For example, I remember one time a client made a rather intricate scene in the Sandtray, but didn't include any people. When I asked the client if she wants to find a piece to represent her and include it in the scene, she pointed to the row boat that was next to a rock in the water and said, "I did already. That's me, and the water is you, and I don't know who the rock is yet." The client didn't need a human figurine that looked identical to her, she actually was able to represent what was going on for her using symbolism which was a fantastic form of expression for her.

Similarly, when you consider the size of the Sandtray that you put into your office, you don't need to get hung up about purchasing or building a very large one. You may worry, "But what if there's not enough room for my clients to create the scene that they want. Again, in this situation as well, clients will spontaneously get creative and find ways of making it work by either crunching it in and making meaning of it, or using space that is out of the box, which may also bring up additional meaning to them. Most therapists would never give a client a 5-hour session twice a week because the client needs more time. Instead, the client is faced with having to pace herself and budget the time available to take maximum advantage of the session time. The same budgeting is true when considering the quantity of items and size of the Sandtray.

To make it easy on you, I've compiled a list of minimum items that will give you a rich inventory to use for many sandtray sessions. For at least some of the items below, you should consider buying several quantities.

There are five main categories of items:

1. Environmental and Structural Items
   a. Bridge
   b. Tree
   c. Rocks
   d. House
   e. Fences
2. People and Characters
   a. Family Representations
   b. Baby
   c. Protectors and Community Figures
   d. Heroes- such as Superman, Superwoman, Wonderwoman, Batman
   e. Mythical Representations
   f. Military
   g. Any human figurine
3. Transportation and machines
   a. Cars
   b. Trucks
   c. Construction Trucks
   d. Airplanes
   e. Army related vehicles
   f. Row Boat
   g. Motorcycle
4. Animals and creatures
   a. Horses
   b. Lion
   c. Butterfly
   d. Snake

e. Dragon
   f. Wild Animals
   g. Domesticated Animals
   h. Farm Animals
5. Things
   a. Locks
   b. Keys
   c. Handcuffs
   d. Sword
   e. Treasure Chest
   f. Inspiration stones- These are super popular and useful
   g. Gems
   h. Valuable coins/ Money
   i. Compass
   j. Trophy
   k. Light / candle
   l. Skull and/or Skeleton
   m. Religious items or symbols
   n. Sea shells

# Appendix

## (Excerpted from Making Therapy Work: A Client's Guide to Healing and Growing In Therapy)[4]

## CLIENTS: THE UNSUNG HEROES OF THERAPY

Congratulations! You made the decision to start your therapeutic journey, and that means you are on your way to a better life.

Once upon a time, there was a stigma about going to therapy. You had to be crazy to go to a therapist. Nowadays, you'd have to be crazy not to! Therapy is about healing pain, developing your emotional world, facing life transitions, and growing in confidence. If you are seeking to improve your life, therapy can provide the setting and structure to pursue your ideal life, break through issues that are blocking you, and achieve an overall greater sense of well-being!

How can you get the most out of therapy so that you can live a life that's real, vibrant and connected to people you love and who love you?

As a therapist, I've been educated by hundreds of hours of training, supervision, and consultation. I discovered that despite all my training and education about how to be a good therapist, no one was educating my clients and helping them make the most of their

---

[4] Making Therapy Work, written by this author, is available on Amazon and is written for clients.

therapy.

Once I realized this, I began to incorporate this education as an integral part of the work that I do with my clients. The feedback I received from my clients was always positive and I found that it also supported the process of their therapy to progress and ultimately help them get the most from their therapy.

One session, a client and I were having a discussion about the process of therapy and her contribution as a client. At the end of the rewarding discussion, she said to me, "How come no one ever told me this before?" This client had a history of going to many therapists and no one had ever engaged her in this kind of discussion, explaining to her the important role of the client.

I challenged her and asked, "How come you never researched it yourself?" She responded that, in fact, she had looked into it many times, but never found anything clear and helpful on the topic. After the session, I did my own research and saw that she was correct. There was a gaping hole in the available resources that left clients neglected of guidance on how to make their therapy effective and explain how it works.

I was then inspired to write this book for all my future clients, and for anyone else who was braving through the journey of therapy.

How do you know if your therapist is any good? Is my therapy working? Am I doing it right or wasting my time? What exactly is therapy?

These are some of the common questions that many people consider when they begin therapy. To be sure, research shows that therapy does work. It helps make people's lives better, and more satisfying. But the reality is, therapy still seems to be working better for some people than others. Why some people seem to fly by with success in therapy while others don't benefit at all? How can you be sure to be making the most of your therapy?

I began to do some research about what type of therapies and therapists offer the best and most efficient services, and what I found was truly eye-opening. While it's true that there are some therapists that are better than others, and some therapies that are better than others, it's also true that **there are some clients that 'do therapy' more effectively than others.**

Some people just seem to be more effective participants in therapy than others. There are certain clients that seem to catch on very quickly in the therapy process and participate and reap benefits; while there are others who either catch on slowly or all-together don't get it.

According to eminent psychotherapy researcher Arthur Bohart, the conclusion of extensive analyses of what works in therapy is that *the Client, not the therapist, plays the biggest role in how well therapy works.* In fact, internationally recognized expert in the field of psychotherapy research Dr. David Orlinsky (2004) concludes that the client is the "most determinant of outcome" in therapy.

In other words, whether you go to the most experienced and trained therapist or the newest and most novice, what you as the Client do in therapy and how you approach your own work makes the biggest difference!

This is great news for you because it means you really are in a position to play a positive role in getting the recovery and help you want. Discovering this research was even more encouraging for me to write this book and make it available to everyone in therapy.

In this book, you will learn how to make the most of your therapy so that you can grow, change, and live a meaningful and full life. Good therapy improves the quality of life, and when you know how to **make therapy work**, then everything in life gets better!

Let me show you how!

# Sandtray Therapy

Michael Elliot

# ABOUT THE AUTHOR

Michael Elliot, MA is an author and Therapist specializing in the treatment of trauma. His other book *Making Therapy Work: A Client's Guide to Healing and Growing In* Therapy, has received praise from both Clinicians and Clients. As a therapist, he works with patients suffering from concerns ranging from low self-esteem to addictions and Complex Trauma. He is in private practice in Baltimore, MD and can be reached at MakingTherapyWork@gmail.com.

Michael Elliot

Made in the USA
Monee, IL
29 September 2019